ON LINE

724.09

ER
Molte
Molter, Carey

Live Lions Live on Land

Live Lions
Live on Land

Carey Molter

Published by SandCastle™, an imprint of ABDO Publishing Company, 4940 Viking Drive, Edina, Minnesota 55435.

Copyright © 2002 by Abdo Consulting Group, Inc. International copyrights reserved in all countries. No part of this book may be reproduced in any form without written permission from the publisher. SandCastle™ is a trademark and logo of ABDO Publishing Company. Printed in the United States.

Cover and interior photo credits: Brand X Pictures, Corel, Digital Vision, Eyewire Images, Carey Molter, PhotoDisc, Rubberball Productions, Stockbyte

Library of Congress Cataloging-in-Publication Data

Molter, Carey, 1973-
　　Live lions live on land / Carey Molter.
　　　　p. cm. -- (Homographs)
　　Includes index.
　　Summary: Photographs and simple text introduce homophones, words with different meanings that are spelled the same but sound different.
　　ISBN 1-57765-795-0
　　1. English language--Homonyms--Juvenile literature. [1. English language--Homonyms.] I. Title.

PE1595 .M67 2002
428.1--dc21

2001053321

The SandCastle concept, content, and reading method have been reviewed and approved by a national advisory board including literacy specialists, librarians, elementary school teachers, early childhood education professionals, and parents.

Let Us Know

After reading the book, SandCastle would like you to tell us your stories about reading. What is your favorite page? Was there something hard that you needed help with? Share the ups and downs of learning to read. We want to hear from you! To get posted on the ABDO Publishing Company Web site, send us email at:

sandcastle@abdopub.com

About SandCastle™

Nonfiction books for the beginning reader

- Basic concepts of phonics are incorporated with integrated language methods of reading instruction. Most words are short, and phrases, letter sounds, and word sounds are repeated.

- Book levels are based on the ATOS™ for Books formula. Other considerations for readability include the number of words in each sentence, the number of characters in each word, and word lists based on curriculum frameworks.

- Full-color photography reinforces word meanings and concepts.

- "Words I Can Read" list at the end of each book teaches basic elements of grammar, helps the reader recognize the words in the text, and builds vocabulary.

- Reading levels are indicated by the number of flags on the castle.

SandCastle uses the following definitions for this series:

- Homographs: words that are spelled the same but sound different and have different meanings. *Easy memory tip: "-graph"= same look*

- Homonyms: words that are spelled and sound the same but have different meanings. *Easy memory tip: "-nym"= same name*

- Homophones: words that sound alike but are spelled differently and have different meanings. *Easy memory tip: "-phone"= sound alike*

Look for more SandCastle books in these three reading levels:

Level 1
(one flag)

Level 2
(two flags)

Level 3
(three flags)

Grades Pre-K to K
5 or fewer words per page

Grades K to 1
5 to 10 words per page

Grades 1 to 2
10 to 15 words per page

Note: Many of the pages in this book have fewer than 10 words due to the difficulty of the subject matter.

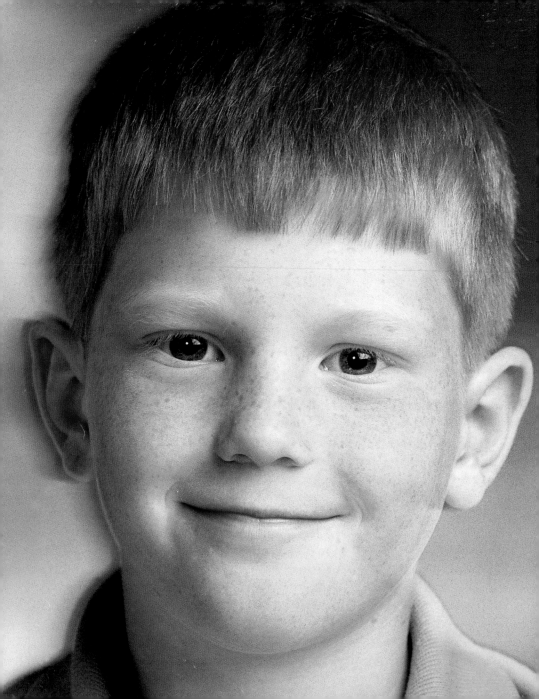

Homographs are words that are spelled the same but sound different and have different meanings.

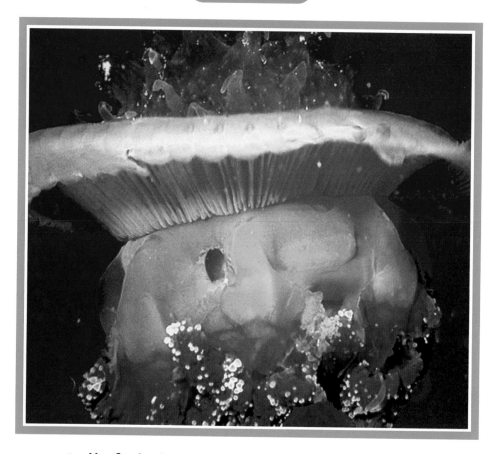

Jellyfish live in the water.

I like to watch live football games.

We are careful not to tear our paper dolls.

Bob has a tear on his cheek.

Jess likes to record new things.

This photo album is a record of my family.

These girls share the umbrella.

They have separate treats.

Ron and Lara are always together.

They hardly ever separate.

Does are female deer.

These graze in the meadow.

Clark does his homework every night.

He sits at the kitchen table.

Grandpa will sow these seeds to grow corn.

A female pig is called a sow.

(KON-trakt)

You must read a **contract** carefully before signing it.

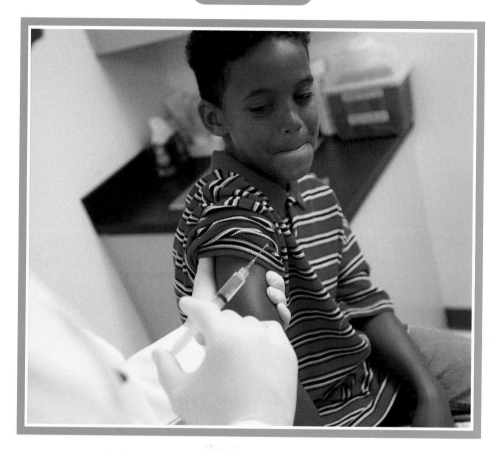

Todd gets a shot so he does not contract an illness.

Boyd dove into the pool for the ball.

What kind of bird is this?

(dove)

Words I Can Read

Nouns

A noun is a person, place, or thing

album (AL-buhm) p. 11
ball (BAWL) p. 20
bird (BURD) p. 21
cheek (CHEEK) p. 9
contract (KON-trakt)
  p. 18
corn (KORN) p. 16
deer (DIHR) p. 14
does (DOHZ) p. 14
dolls (DOLZ) p. 8
dove (DUHV) p. 21
family (FAM-uh-lee)
  p. 11
football (FUT-bal) p. 7
games (GAYMZ) p. 7
girls (GURLZ) p. 12

homework
  (HOME-wurk) p. 15
homographs
  (HOM-uh-grafss) p. 5
illness (IL-ness) p. 19
jellyfish (JEL-ee-fish)
  p. 6
kind (KINDE) p. 21
kitchen (KICH-uhn)
  p. 15
meadow (MED-oh)
  p. 14
meanings (MEE-ningz)
  p. 5
night (NITE) p. 15
paper (PAY-pur) p. 8

photo (FOH-toh) p. 11
pig (PIG) p. 17
pool (POOL) p. 20
record (REK-urd) p. 11
seeds (SEEDZ) p. 16
shot (SHOT) p. 19
sow (SOU) p. 17
table (TAY-buhl) p. 15
tear (TIHR) p. 9
things (THINGZ) p. 10
treats (TREETSS) p. 12
umbrella
  (uhm-BREL-uh) p. 12
water (WAW-tur) p. 6
words (WURDZ) p. 5

Proper Nouns

A proper noun is the name of a person, place, or thing

Bob (BOB) p. 9
Boyd (BOID) p. 20
Clark (KLARK) p. 15

Grandpa
  (GRAND-pah) p. 16
Jess (JESS) p. 10

Lara (LAR-uh) p. 13
Ron (RON) p. 13
Todd (TOD) p. 19

Pronouns
A pronoun is a word that replaces a noun

he (HEE) pp. 15, 19
I (EYE) p. 7
it (IT) p. 18

these (THEEZ) p. 14
they (THAY) pp. 12, 13
this (THISS) p. 21

we (WEE) p. 8
what (WUHT) p. 21
you (YOO) p. 18

Verbs
A verb is an action or being word

are (AR) pp. 5, 8, 13, 14
called (KAWLD) p. 17
contract (kuhn-TRAKT) p. 19
does (DUHZ) pp. 15, 19
dove (DOHV) p. 20
gets (GETSS) p. 19
graze (GRAYZ) p. 14
grow (GROH) p. 16
has (HAZ) p. 9

have (HAV) pp. 5, 12
is (IZ) pp. 11, 17, 21
like (LIKE) p. 7
likes (LIKESS) p. 10
live (LIV) p. 6
must (MUHST) p. 18
read (REED) p. 18
record (ri-KORD) p. 10
separate (SEP-uh-rate) p. 13

share (SHAIR) p. 12
signing (SINE-ing) p. 18
sits (SITSS) p. 15
sound (SOUND) p. 5
sow (SOH) p. 16
spelled (SPELD) p. 5
tear (TAIR) p. 8
watch (WOCH) p. 7
will (WIL) p. 16

Adjectives
An adjective describes something

careful (KAIR-fuhl) p. 8
different (DIF-ur-uhnt) p. 5
every (EV-ree) p. 15
female (FEE-male) pp. 14, 17

his (HIZ) pp. 9, 15
live (LIVE) p. 7
my (MYE) p. 11
new (NOO) p. 10
our (OUR) p. 8
same (SAYM) p. 5

separate (SEP-ur-it) p. 12
these (THEEZ) pp. 12, 16
this (THISS) p. 11

Adverbs

An adverb tells how, when, or where something happens

always (AWL-waze)
p. 13

carefully
(KAIR-fuhl-ee) p. 18

ever (EV-ur) p. 13

hardly (HARD-lee)
p. 13

same (SAYM) p. 5

together
(tuh-GETH-ur) p. 13